Dedicated to my students.

- Mrs. Dorcely

   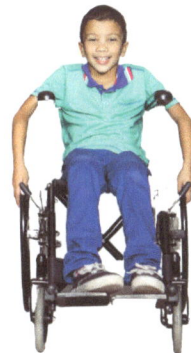

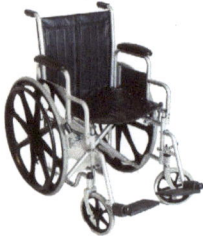

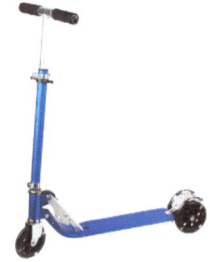

This book belongs to:

_____

Ms. Pat brings different toys and pictures to class. She says, "Who can guess the question of the day?"

One student says,
"How do you get to school?"

"You are correct," says Ms. Pat.

How do you get to school?

Some students walk to school.

Some students get to school on bicycles.

Some students get to school on scooters.

Some students get to school on motorcycles.

Some students get to school
on a yellow school bus.

Some students go to school on a city bus.

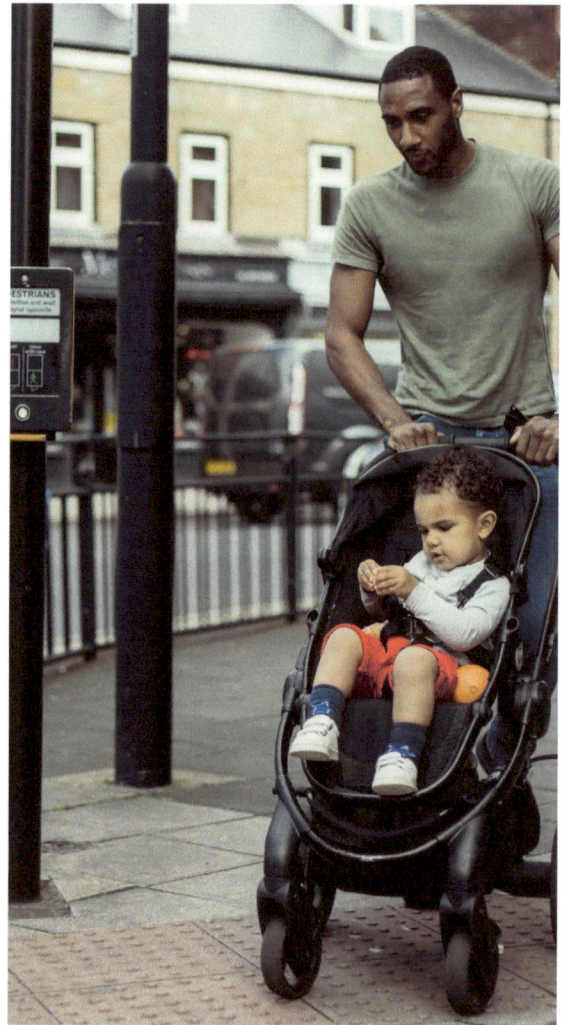

Some students get to school in strollers.

Some students get to school on the train.

Some students get to school in cars.

Some students get to school in a taxi.

Some students get to school on a ferry.

Some students get to school on skateboards.

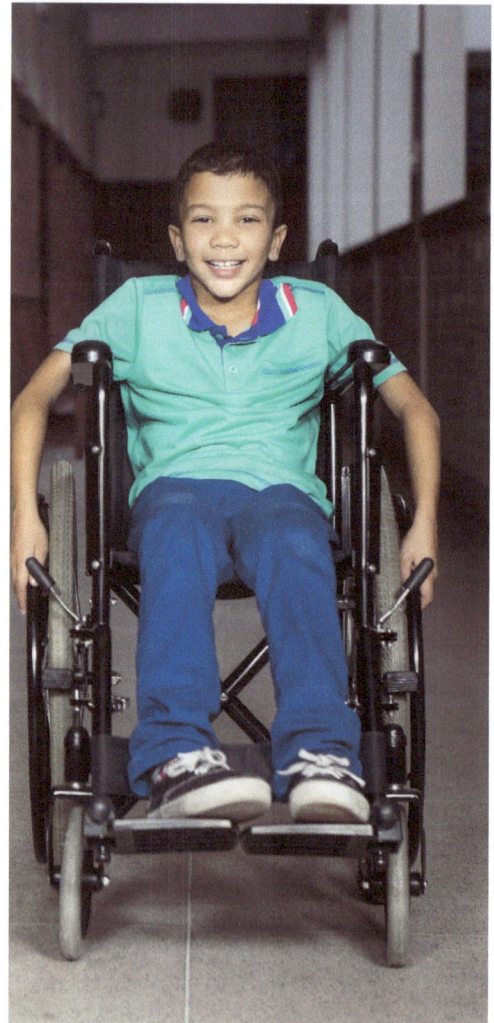

Some students get to school in wheelchairs.

Some students get to school
on roller skates.

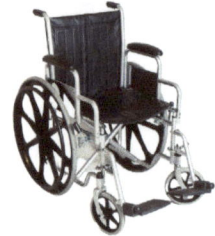

How do you get to school?

Color the pictures of how you get to school!

train

taxi

scooter

walk

skateboard

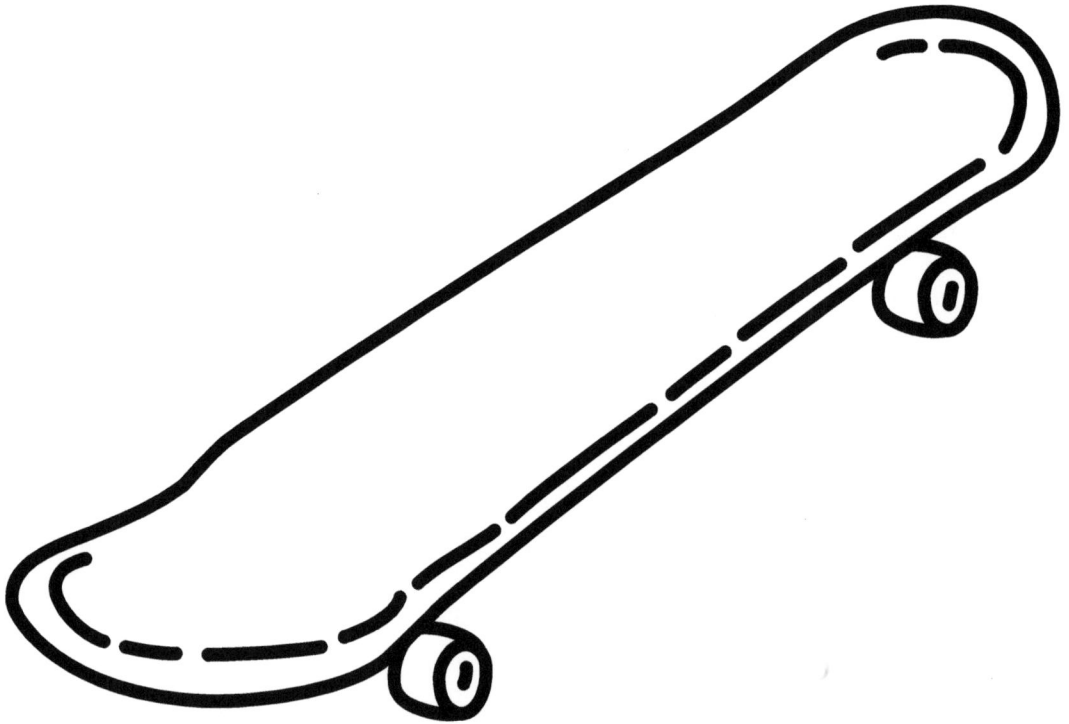

stroller

school bus

wheelchair

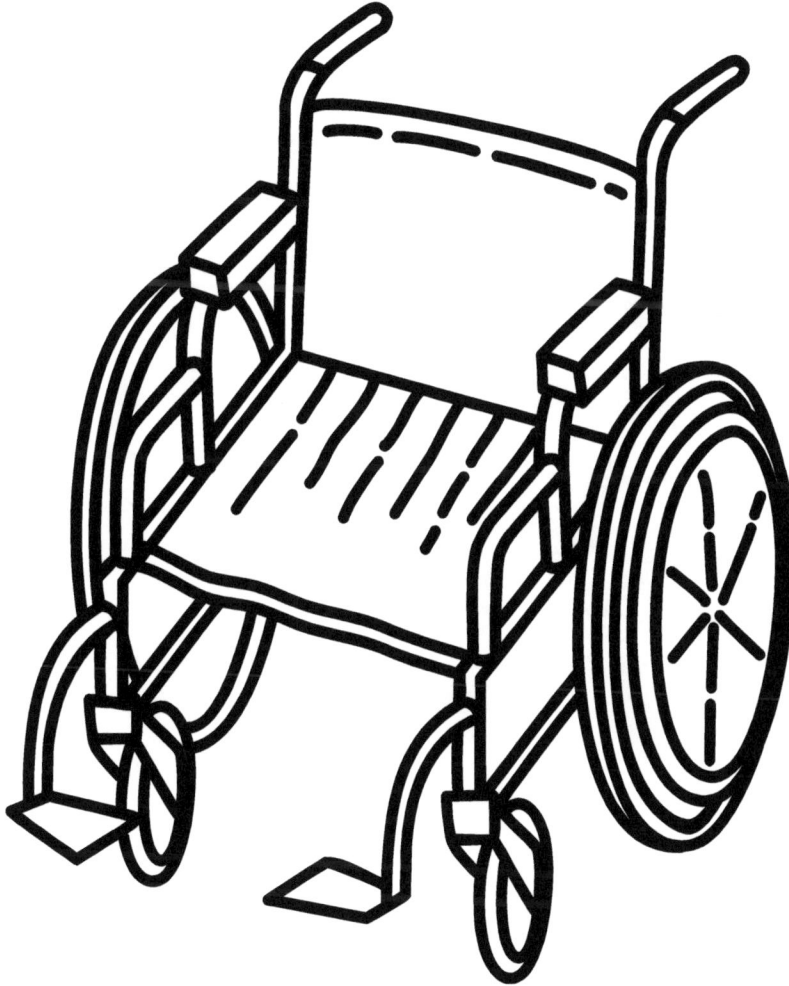

motorcycle

car

ferry

roller skates

Write your name or put your picture on the chart to show how you get to school.

Write your name or put your picture on the chart to show how you get to school.

Write your name or put your picture on the chart to show how you get to school.

Write your name or put your picture on the chart to show how you get to school.

Draw a picture of how you get to school.

walk

bicycle

ferry

motorcycle

skateboard

car

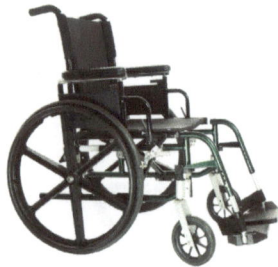

wheelchair

scooter

 **school bus**

 **bus**

 **train**

 **stroller**

taxi

roller skates

school

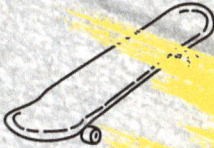

How Do You Get to School?

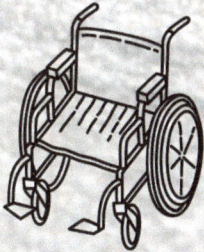

www.ingramcontent.com/pod-product-compliance
Lightning Source LLC
LaVergne TN
LVHW072130070426
835513LV00002B/50